Newbridge Discovery Links®

BIG DIGS

Meish Goldish

Newbridge

A Haights Cross Communications Company

Big Digs
ISBN: 1-58273-721-5

Program Author: Dr. Brenda Parkes
Content Reviewer: Michael Haviken, Construction Project Superintendent, New York, NY
Teacher Reviewer: Jennifer Goldenberg, Stevenson Elementary School, Burbank, CA

Written by Meish Goldish
Editorial and Design Assistance by Curriculum Concepts

Newbridge Educational Publishing
333 East 38th Street, New York, NY 10016
www.newbridgeonline.com

Cover Photograph: A big dig in progress
Table of Contents Photograph: Checking meter in the power plant at Hoover Dam

Photo Credits
Cover: J. B. Boykin/The Stock Market; Table of Contents page: Robert Maass/CORBIS; page 4: Nubar
Alexanian/Stock Boston; pages 6–7: Danny Lehman/CORBIS; page 9: CORBIS; page 10: Underwood
& Underwood/CORBIS; page 11: (inset) CORBIS, (background) AFP/CORBIS; page 13: Dave G.
Houser/CORBIS; pages 14–15: Kevin Fleming/CORBIS; page 16: United States Department of the
Interior, Bureau of Reclamation; page 19: Lake County Museum/CORBIS; page 20: Marc Granger/
CORBIS; page 21: Robert Maass/CORBIS; pages 22–23: Bill Horsman/Stock Boston; page 25: Andy
Ryan; page 27: Andy Ryan; page 28: Central Artery/Tunnel Project; page 29: Central Artery/Tunnel
Project; page 30: Nubar Alexanian/Stock Boston; page 31: Underwood & Underwood/CORBIS

Maps/Illustrations by Mike DiGiorgio pages 8, 12, 17, 18, 24; Steve Stankiewicz, page 26

10 9 8 7 6 5 4 3

Table of Contents

Why Dig?

Why would anyone want to dig a deep trench almost all the way across an entire country? Why would anyone want to dig tunnels in the desert and into canyon walls? And why would anyone want to dig for over twenty years in the middle of a busy city? You're about to find out!

In this book, you will learn about three major building projects of the last 100 years. They are the Panama Canal, Hoover Dam, and Boston's Big Dig. You will discover how and why each structure was built, and what special problems had to be overcome to do the job.

Are you ready for some "big digs"? Good! Then dig in!

Digging is the first step, and careful construction comes next for projects such as canals, dams, tunnels, and bridges.

A Shortcut Through the Jungle

So, why would anyone want to dig a deep trench almost all the way across an entire country? The answer can be found in the story of the Panama Canal.

Since the 1500s, explorers and travelers had dreamed of cutting through Central America to create a waterway, or **canal**. Such a canal would be a shortcut between the Atlantic and Pacific Oceans.

By the 1890s, the United States stretched from sea to sea. People wanted a safer, faster, and easier way to go back and forth between coasts. Some people wanted to travel to see family, some were looking for adventure, and many more were doing business. The long trip by sea or overland was extremely dangerous. Along the way people often became ill, or even died.

Facing Problems

In 1904, the United States decided to build that canal. President Theodore Roosevelt was the driving force behind the United States' efforts to build the Panama Canal. He knew there were serious problems to be faced, but he also had confidence that they would be solved.

The first problem that had to be solved was the mosquitoes that carried terrible diseases such as malaria and yellow fever. From 1882 to 1889, the French had

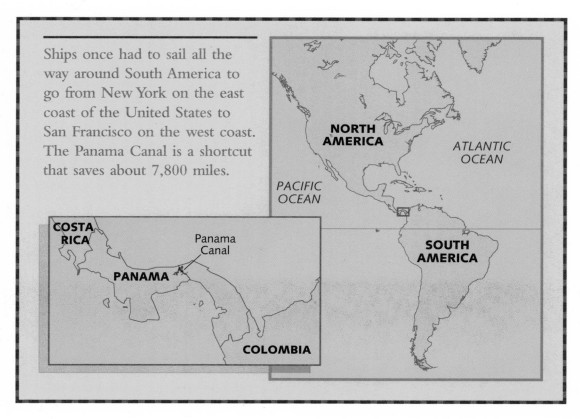

Ships once had to sail all the way around South America to go from New York on the east coast of the United States to San Francisco on the west coast. The Panama Canal is a shortcut that saves about 7,800 miles.

NORTH AMERICA

ATLANTIC OCEAN

PACIFIC OCEAN

SOUTH AMERICA

COSTA RICA

Panama Canal

PANAMA

COLOMBIA

About 75,000 workers from 97 countries helped to build the canal. They worked long, backbreaking hours in often dangerous conditions. Temperatures could reach as high as 130°F.

tried to build a canal in Panama, but the diseases that workers caught while working in the jungle made the project a tragic failure. Before the U.S. project began, workers spent two years draining swamps, clearing brush, and cutting grass where mosquitoes swarmed. By 1906, yellow fever was nearly eliminated in the area. Other diseases also decreased.

Now the real work could get underway. Roosevelt chose George Goethals, an army engineer, to supervise the building of the canal. Several different engineers had already studied the area and saw that the Chagres River flowed across a large part of Panama. It was decided that the river basin would serve as the best route for the canal.

But two new problems arose. First, the Chagres often flooded during heavy rainfall, and that could delay the digging of the canal. Second, what would workers do with the tons of dirt taken from the basin?

Twenty-two major landslides occurred during the digging. In 1913, with that part of the job nearly done, there was a huge landslide. Supervisor David Gaillard and his crew had to dig out all over again. Later, the passage was named the Gaillard Cut in his honor.

An important part of the project was building locks along the canal. The walls of each lock are the height of a six-story building and the length of a city block. The inset shows a worker inside an 18-foot-high structure at Gatun Locks construction site.

Finding Solutions

One answer could solve both problems. Goethals decided to build a **dam** using the **excavated** dirt. The dam would stop the river's flow and create a long, high lake for ships to sail on from the Atlantic to the Pacific Ocean.

Thousands of workers began digging out the Chagres River basin. They used the dirt to create

Gatun Dam, which blocked and controlled the flow of the river. The water filled up behind the dam to create the 24-mile-long Gatun Lake.

One last problem had to be solved. The newly created Gatun Lake was 85 feet higher than the Atlantic Ocean. How would ships reach it? The answer was to build locks—a series of water elevators—to raise and lower ships to different water levels.

In 1914, the Panama Canal was finally completed. In August, the *Cristobal* made history by being the first ship to officially travel through the canal. The locks worked perfectly then, as they still do today.

Each lock is like a big tub full of water, but the tubs have gates that open to let water and ships in or out. When water pours into a lock, it moves the ship higher. When water pours out of a lock, it moves the ship lower. In this way, ships pass from the lower level of the oceans to the higher level of Gatun Lake. Because of the twists and turns along the way, a ship that enters the canal from the Atlantic side leaves the canal 27 miles east of where it started! You can see this on the map on page 8.

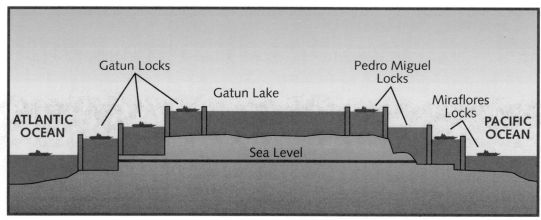

Every time a ship passes through the canal, 52 million gallons of fresh water are used from Gatun Lake! To conserve water, smaller ships often travel through the locks together. Today, about 1,000 ships pass through the canal each month.

BIG Facts

- The French engineer who oversaw the first attempt to build the canal was Ferdinand de Lesseps. Twenty-two thousand men died and nearly 300 million dollars were wasted on the job that never got done.

- Before the Panama Canal was built, a ship sailed 13,000 miles from New York to San Francisco. After the canal was built, the trip was less than 5,200 miles.

- First opened in 1914, the Panama Canal was controlled by the United States. Since 1999 it has been owned and operated by Panama.

Taming a Wild River

Now, what about tunneling through the desert and canyon walls? Why would anyone want to do that? The story of Hoover Dam explains why.

In 1928, the U.S. Congress voted to build a dam on the Colorado River. The dam would prevent the river from flooding homes and farms during periods of heavy rain, by holding back the river water in a lake or **reservoir**, and letting a controlled amount flow through the dam. It would also store water for farmland **irrigation** when the weather was too dry. And the dam would generate electrical power for cities and towns in the area.

Frank Crowe, an engineer, headed the project to build Hoover Dam. He knew that it would be difficult.

Before the project could begin, roads, railroads, and housing for workers had to be built near the dam site which was located in an uninhabited area of the desert. Water and power lines had to be run to the area. In time, a whole town was created in the desert to support the building of the dam.

At the height of the Great Depression, when jobs were hard to find, men willingly worked seven days a week to construct Hoover Dam. Scaling walls and digging tunnels were often dangerous and unhealthy jobs, but such work beat starvation.

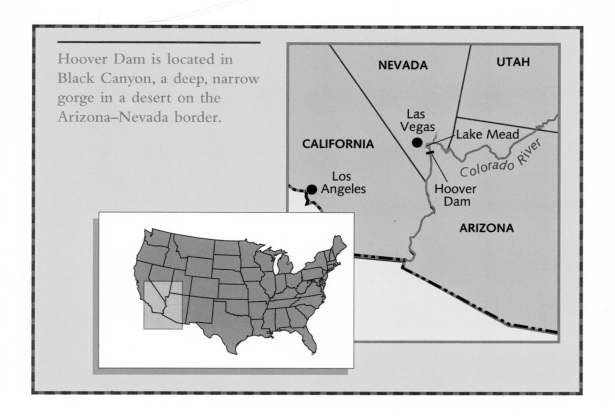

Hoover Dam is located in Black Canyon, a deep, narrow gorge in a desert on the Arizona–Nevada border.

NEVADA

UTAH

Las Vegas

Lake Mead

CALIFORNIA

Colorado River

Los Angeles

Hoover Dam

ARIZONA

River Reroute

One more problem remained before workers could begin construction of the dam. The Colorado River flowed over the place where the dam was to be built. The riverbed had to be dry for crews to work there. What would be done with the river while the dam was being built?

Crowe's solution was to **divert** the Colorado River so it flowed elsewhere during construction. Work crews dynamited through canyon walls to create four tunnels, each about 4,000 feet long. During the job, many workers died in the tunnels due to extreme heat, rock slides, or falls from the cliff walls.

After two years, the tunnels were ready. The river now flowed through them, leaving the canyon and riverbed dry for workers to build the dam.

Higher and Higher

In 1932, crews prepared the foundation for the dam. They dug up the riverbed until they struck bedrock. Railway cars carried away the mud and gravel that had been dug up.

The dam works by changing the way water flows. Intake towers fill up with water and send it into pipes that carry it to the powerhouses where electricity is made, or to pipes for irrigation. Other pipes carry water back to the riverbed.

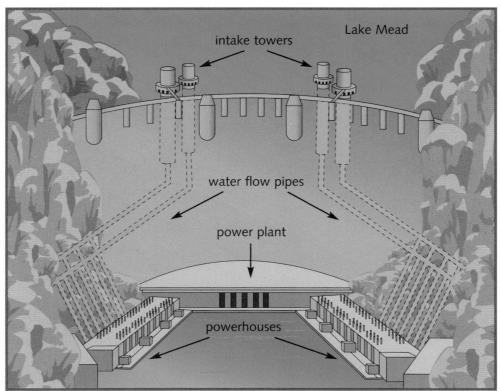

Workers poured concrete into hundreds of blocks, each five feet thick. Cables carried buckets of concrete higher and higher as the dam slowly grew. Pipes in the blocks carried water that cooled the concrete so that it could dry and harden before more concrete was poured.

The dam rose, block by block, to 726 feet in height—as tall as a 50-story building. At the dam's base, the concrete was 660 feet thick—thicker than the length of two football fields put together.

In 1935, construction of the dam was complete. Workers sealed the four tunnels that had diverted the Colorado River during construction. The river returned to its normal course, and the dam now prevented it from flooding the valley.

The large amount of water that backed up behind Hoover Dam formed a huge reservoir called Lake Mead. It is one of the largest artificially created bodies of water in the world.

Watershed Rewards

Once Hoover Dam was finished, it began to provide many benefits for people in Arizona, Nevada, and California. Water from Lake Mead irrigates about a million acres of farmland in the tristate area. The lake also supplies water for Los Angeles, San Diego, Phoenix, Las Vegas, and other cities. It is a great source of recreation for visitors as well.

Hoover Dam also provides those cities with electricity. And of course, the dam controls the river, so it no longer floods farms and towns along its course.

Nine of Hoover Dam's electrical generators are in Arizona and eight are in Nevada. Inside the control room today, workers monitor water levels and electricity flows. You can tour the facility, which is about 35 miles east of Las Vegas, Nevada.

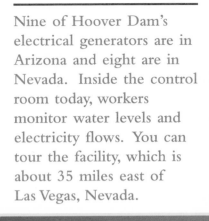

BIG Facts

- Hoover Dam was named for Herbert Hoover, the U.S. president in office while the dam was under construction.

- Hoover Dam weighs over 6,600,000 tons. It has enough concrete to pave a sidewalk that could go all the way around the earth.

- Lake Mead is 115 miles long and 589 feet deep. It holds enough water to cover the entire state of New York with one foot of water.

- The top of Hoover Dam is a concrete road 45 feet wide. About 20,000 vehicles a day drive on the road, linking Arizona and Nevada.

Keeping Up with a Busy City

What reason could anyone have for undertaking a huge digging project in the middle of a busy city? And why dig for so many years?

In the 1980s, commuters in Boston, Massachusetts, faced serious traffic problems. Every day, cars, trucks, buses, and taxis jammed the highways, bridges, and tunnels running through the city.

Boston is built on a harbor and bounded by the Charles River. If more traffic were allowed to move under and over the water, the city could have more space for parks and pedestrians. And traffic could move more easily.

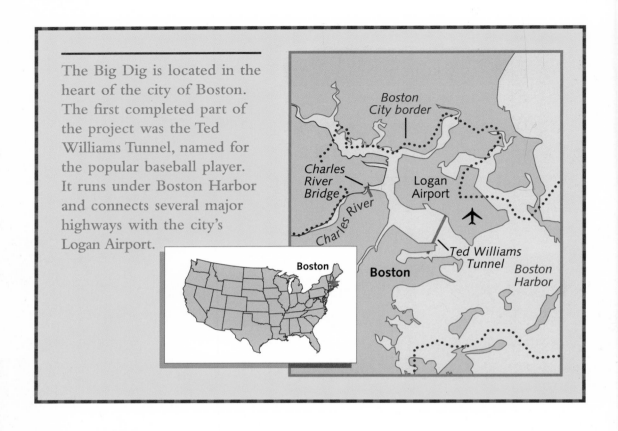

The Big Dig is located in the heart of the city of Boston. The first completed part of the project was the Ted Williams Tunnel, named for the popular baseball player. It runs under Boston Harbor and connects several major highways with the city's Logan Airport.

Boston City border

Charles River Bridge

Logan Airport

Charles River

Ted Williams Tunnel

Boston

Boston Harbor

Boston

In 1982, the city began planning a major building program called the Central Artery/Tunnel Project. Its nickname became the Big Dig. Its goal was to provide new and wider highways and tunnels for the city, plus two bridges carrying 14 lanes of traffic across the Charles River.

A Tubular Tunnel

In 1991, workers began to build a tunnel under Boston Harbor. Construction of the tunnel actually began in Baltimore, Maryland. There, 12 pairs of steel tubes were created, with each tube about 300 feet long and 40 feet in **diameter**. One tube in each pair would hold traffic heading east, while the other would hold traffic heading west.
The tubes were designed so that later they could be fit tightly together to form one long tunnel. In 1993, the completed tubes were floated by **barge** to a pier on Boston's waterfront.

One of the biggest challenges planners had to meet was to do major construction in the midst of a busy, congested city. As the Big Dig went on below the city, subways, cars, bicycles, and pedestrians hurried along as usual.

Sinking to the Bottom

Meanwhile, the world's largest **dredging machine** was digging a trench, or ditch, 50 feet deep in the harbor. The tunnel tubes would eventually rest in this trench at the bottom of the harbor.

The tubes were barged into the harbor. Then, one by one, the tubes were filled with water, sunk, and set into the trench. Workers anchored the tubes and pumped each section dry. Crews lined the tunnel walls with concrete and reinforced them with steel.

Twelve steel sections had to be fit one in front of the other to make the underwater part of the tunnel. Each section is about 300 feet long.

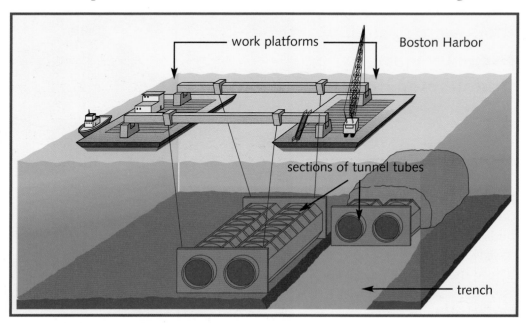

The tunnel grew to 1.6 miles long. Giant fans inside buildings at each end of the tunnel blow in fresh air and draw out fumes.

With the tubes in place, workers added the final touches to the insides of the tunnel. They dug land tunnels as entrances and exits to the underwater tunnel. Then the tubes were connected and sealed to create the long tunnel.

The tunnel opened in 1995. The South Boston waterfront and the airport were connected. But the Big Dig had just begun. There were still bridges and roads to build and parks to complete.

Spanning the River

The Big Dig project includes two bridges connecting Charlestown with downtown Boston. One bridge, named the Leonard P. Zakim Bunker Hill Bridge, is the Big Dig's crown jewel. It is the widest cable-stayed bridge in the world, and the only one built of steel and concrete.

Cable-stayed bridges are also called suspension bridges. This is because the thick cables that run between the bridge's towers and its roadway actually suspend, or hold up, the bridge.

It has two concrete towers, each shaped like an upside-down letter y. The upper level of the bridge has straddle tracks for two mass transit lines. Eight lanes of traffic travel on the lower level. Two more lanes for traffic are **suspended** off either side of the bridge.

When it is completed, the Big Dig will have eased traffic and created many beautiful new parks for everyone in Boston to enjoy.

Throughout the bridge's construction, heavy traffic zoomed past the work site on an elevated highway that will later be torn down.

BIG Facts

- The Central Artery/Tunnel Project is the largest and most complex highway project in U.S. history.

- Fifteen million cubic yards of dirt will be dug up in downtown Boston during the Big Dig. That's enough dirt to fill a football stadium. It will be used to create new public parks.

- The Big Dig should allow 245,000 vehicles to travel through Boston daily, about 50,000 more than could travel before.

Big Improvements

Each of the "big digs" described in this book has been a true problem solver. About 15,000 ships now pass through the Panama Canal each year. This shortcut sharply increased shipping and trade around the world.

Hoover Dam prevents dangerous floods. It also provides water and electricity to millions of homes and businesses in California, Nevada, and Arizona. In addition, Lake Mead is a popular boating and recreation area.

Boston's Big Dig will not only reduce traffic jams, but improve air quality as well. That's because less pollution will be released by cars stuck waiting in traffic jams. New parks will be constructed over covered highways, creating more green space, too.

Think about the ways that canals, dams, tunnels, and bridges benefit you or people you know. You will agree that big digs help our world in big ways!

Glossary

barge: a long, flat boat used to carry heavy loads

canal: a narrow waterway that is usually made by people

dam: a structure built to stop the flow of water, especially rivers

diameter: the distance across the center of a circle

divert: to change the direction in which something is flowing

dredging machine: a machine that digs up mud from the bottom of a body of water

excavated: dug up and removed to create space

irrigation: a system for supplying and controlling the amount of water that is used for crops

reservoir: an artificial lake often used to store water for drinking and irrigation

suspended: held in the air

Websites

Find out more about "big digs" at

www.bigdig.com
www.hooverdam.usbr.gov
www.discovery.com/stories/history/panama/map.html

Index